Reading Yellow Pages

for Students and Teachers

from The KIDS' STUFF™ People

Incentive Publications, Inc.
Nashville, TN.

Special acknowledgement is accorded to

- *The KIDS' STUFF™ People for compiling and organizing the materials included in this publication*
- *Susan Eaddy for the cover design*
- *Sally Sharpe, Editor*

ISBN 0-86530-029-1
Library of Congress Catalog Card Number 87-83365

Table of Contents

SHORT VOWEL WORDS

Short A Words

add	chance	grab	pad	slap
after	clam	grand	pal	slat
ant	clamp	grant	pan	snag
ask	clasp	grass	pant	snap
at	class	had	pass	span
ax	crack	ham	past	splash
back	cramp	hand	pat	stab
bad	crash	handle	plan	stack
bag	dad	hat	plant	stamp
bat	dam	jab	quack	tab
bath	damp	jam	rack	tacks
black	dance	lab	raft	tag
bland	dash	lamb	rag	tan
brand	drab	lamp	ram	task
brass	fact	land	ran	than
cab	fan	last	rang	that
camp	fat	mad	rap	track
can	flag	man	rat	trap
candle	flat	map	sack	trash
cap	gal	mask	sad	vamp
cash	gap	master	sand	van
cast	gas	match	sang	vast
cat	glance	nag	scab	wax
catch	glass	nap	scrap	yam
champ	gnat	pack	slab	

Short E Words

beck	dwell	ledge	quench	them
bed	edge	left	red	then
beg	egg	leg	rent	vent
bell	elbow	less	rest	vest
bench	ever	let	scent	vet
bend	fed	level	sell	vex
bent	fell	men	send	web
best	fence	mend	sent	wed
bet	fetch	mess	shed	wedge
bled	fleck	met	shell	well
blend	fled	neck	shred	went
bless	flesh	nest	sled	wept
bred	fresh	net	sledge	west
cell	gem	never	slept	wet
cent	get	next	smell	when
center	hedge	pebble	sped	wreck
chest	helmet	peck	spell	wrench
clef	help	peg	spend	yell
crest	hem	pen	spent	yelp
deck	hen	pep	stress	yes
dell	jelly	pest	swept	yet
dense	jest	pet	tell	zest
dent	jet	pledge	ten	
desk	kept	press	tent	
dress	led	quell	test	

7

Short I Words

bib	ill	pinch	strip
bid	in	pit	swim
big	inch	rib	thin
bill	jig	rid	thing
bin	kick	rift	this
brick	kid	rig	tickle
bridge	king	rill	till
chick	kiss	rim	tin
chin	knit	rip	tip
dig	lid	risk	twin
dill	lift	ship	twist
dim	limb	shrill	vim
dip	lint	sick	vision
dish	lip	sift	whiff
fib	list	silk	whim
fig	lit	simmer	whip
fill	milk	sin	whiskers
film	miss	sip	whistle
fish	mist	sister	wick
fist	mister	sit	wig
fix	mitt	six	will
grin	nibble	skill	win
grip	nick	slit	wing
hid	nil	spill	wit
hill	nip	split	with
him	pick	stick	wrist
hint	picnic	still	yip
his	pig	sting	zip
hit	pin	stitch	

Short O Words

block	cost	hock	monster	shod
bog	cot	hog	mop	shop
bomb	crock	hop	moss	shot
bond	crop	hot	moth	slob
boss	cross	job	nod	slop
bottle	dock	jot	not	slosh
box	dodge	knob	on	slot
broth	dog	knock	ox	smock
chop	doll	knot	plod	smog
clock	dollar	lock	plop	snob
clod	dot	lodge	plot	sob
clog	drop	loft	pocket	sock
clop	flop	log	pod	song
closet	fog	lollipop	pond	spot
cloth	fond	lop	pop	stock
cob	forgot	loss	pot	stop
cock	fox	lost	rob	top
cod	frost	lot	rock	toss
cog	gloss	mob	rod	
common	gob	mock	rot	
con	got	mod	rotten	
cop	hobble	mom	shock	

Short U Words

bluff	fuzz	plum
blunt	glum	plunge
blush	glut	plus
brunch	grub	pulp
buck	grudge	pump
bud	gruff	punch
buff	grump	pup
bug	gull	rub
bum	gum	ruffle
bump	gun	rug
bun	gush	rum
bunch	gut	run
bundle	gutter	rung
bunt	hub	rush
bus	huff	rust
but	hug	rut
buzz	hull	skull
clump	hum	skunk
clutch	humble	slug
crumb	hump	slum
crunch	hunch	slump
crust	hung	sprung
cub	hunt	struck
cuff	husk	stun
cull	hut	stunt
cup	jug	sun
cut	jump	sung
drudge	just	sunk
drug	jut	swung
drum	luck	truck
duck	lug	trunk
dug	lull	trust
dull	lump	tub
dumb	lunch	tuck
dump	lung	tug
dusk	muck	tusk
dust	mud	ugly
fluff	mug	umbrella
flung	mull	uncle
flush	munch	under
fluster	mush	unjust
fudge	must	until
fun	null	up
fund	nut	us
fuss	pluck	

LONG VOWEL WORDS

Long A Words (Silent E)

ace	cave	glade	mistake	shape
agape	chase	glaze	name	skate
age	crate	grace	nape	slate
ale	crave	grade	pace	slave
amaze	date	grape	page	snake
ape	daze	grate	pave	space
ate	deface	grave	place	spade
babe	disgrace	graze	plane	stage
bake	drake	hale	plate	stake
bale	drape	hate	quake	stale
base	engage	haze	race	state
bathe	enrage	jade	rage	stave
blame	evade	knave	rake	take
blaze	exhale	lace	rape	tale
behave	face	lake	rate	tame
brace	fade	lame	rave	tape
brake	fake	lane	sage	thane
brave	fame	late	sake	trace
cage	fate	lathe	sale	trade
cake	flake	mace	same	vale
came	flame	made	sane	vane
cane	gale	make	save	wade
cape	game	male	scrape	wage
case	gate	mane	shade	
	gave	mate	shake	
	gaze	maze	shame	

Long I Words (Silent E)

abide	grime	price	strive
advice	gripe	prime	swipe
advise	hive	prize	thrice
arrive	ice	rice	thrive
aside	ire	rife	tile
beside	kite	rile	time
bide	knife	ripe	tire
bile	lice	rise	tribe
bite	life	rite	tripe
bribe	lime	scribe	twice
bride	line	shine	vice
brine	live	shire	vile
chide	mice	shrine	vine
chime	mile	sire	vise
chive	mime	size	while
cite	mine	slice	whine
crime	mire	slime	white
fife	mite	smile	wide
file	nice	spice	wife
fine	nine	splice	wine
fire	pile	stile	wipe
five	pine	strife	wire
glide	pipe	stripe	wise

Long O Words (Silent E)

bode	grope	rode
bone	hole	rope
broke	home	rose
choke	hone	rote
chose	hope	rove
chrome	hose	scope
clone	hove	slope
close	joke	smoke
clothe	lobe	smote
clove	lone	sole
coke	lope	stoke
cone	mode	stole
cope	mole	stone
cove	mope	stove
crone	node	strobe
dole	nose	strode
dome	note	stroke
dope	phone	those
dose	poke	throne
dote	pole	tone
doze	pope	tote
drone	pose	vote
drove	probe	woke
froze	prone	yoke
globe	quote	zone
	robe	

Long U Words (Silent E)

brute	dude	huge	prune	spruce
butte	duke	jute	puke	tube
chute	dune	mule	pure	tune
crude	dupe	mute	rule	yule
cube	flute	nude	ruse	
cute	fume	prude		

Final Y

Long E					Long I
					buy
alley	factory	hockey	lucky	quickly	by
army	fairy	honey	memory	rocky	cry
baby	family	hungry	money	stingy	dry
bunny	fancy	hurry	mystery	study	fly
bury	funny	ivory	naughty	surgery	fry
busy	furry	ivy	navy	taffy	my
canary	fury	jockey	nursery	tiny	ply
city	glory	journey	party	twenty	pry
country	grocery	jury	penny	ugly	shy
county	happy	lady	plenty	very	sky
drowsy	hardy	lazy	pony	weary	sly
easy	heavy	liberty	poppy	zany	spry
					spy
					sty
					try
					why
					wry

VOWEL DIGRAPHS

-AI-(long a)

aid	drain	lain	quail	tail
aide	fail	maid	quaint	taint
ail	fain	mail	raid	trail
aim	faint	maim	rail	train
bail	faith	main	rain	trait
bait	flail	maize	raise	twain
braid	frail	nail	sail	vain
brain	gaily	paid	saint	waif
braise	gain	pail	slain	wail
chain	gait	pain	snail	wain
chaise	grain	paint	staid	waist
claim	hail	plain	stain	wait
daily	jail	plait	strain	waive
dainty	laid	praise	strait	

-AY-(long a)

bay	flay	lay	say	stay
bray	fray	may	slay	stray
clay	gay	nay	splay	tray
crayon	gray	pay	spray	way
day	hay	play		
dray	jay	ray		

-EA-(long e)

beach	crease	heal	peach	seat
bead	deal	heap	peak	sneak
beak	dean	heat	peal	speak
beam	decease	heave	peat	squeak
bean	decrease	knead	plea	squeal
beast	disease	lead	plead	steal
beat	dream	leaf	please	steam
bleach	each	leak	pleat	streak
bleak	eagle	lean	preach	tea
bleat	ease	leap	reach	teach
breach	east	least	read	teak
cease	eat	leave	real	team
cheap	feast	meal	ream	treat
clean	feat	mean	reap	tweak
cleat	freak	meat	scream	veal
cleave	gleam	neat	sea	weak
creak	glean	pea	seal	yeast
cream	grease	peace	seam	zeal

-EE-(long e)

bee	feed	keen	screen	steel
beech	feel	knee	seed	steep
beep	feet	lee	seek	steeple
between	flee	leech	seem	street
bleed	fleece	leek	seen	teem
breech	fleet	meek	seep	teeth
breed	free	meet	sheen	thee
breeze	freed	need	sheep	three
cheek	freeze	peek	sheet	tree
cheese	geese	peel	sleep	tweed
creed	glee	peep	sleet	weed
creek	greed	peeve	sleeve	weep
creep	green	preen	sneeze	wheel
deed	greet	queen	speech	wheeze
deem	heed	reed	speed	
deep	heel	reek	spleen	
eel	jeep	reel	spree	
fee	keel	screech	squeeze	

-OA-(long o)

afloat	croak	load	oaken	shoat
bloat	float	loaf	oat	soak
boast	foal	loafer	oath	soap
boat	foam	loam	poach	throat
broach	gloaming	loan	poacher	toad
cloak	gloat	loath	roach	toast
coach	goad	loathe	road	toaster
coal	goal	loaves	roam	whoa
coast	goat	moan	roan	
coaster	groan	moat	roast	
coat	groat	oaf	roaster	
coax	hoax	oak	shoal	

13

-OO-(boot)

bloom	hoot	scoop
boom	loom	shoot
boost	loop	sloop
booster	loose	smooth
boot	loot	snooze
brood	mood	spoof
cool	moose	spool
coop	noon	spoon
doom	noose	stool
drool	pool	stoop
droop	proof	swoop
food	roof	too
fool	room	toot
gloom	roost	tooth
goose	rooster	troop
groom	root	whoop
hoop	school	zoo

-OO-(book)

book	good	poor
boor	hood	rook
brook	hoof	shook
cook	hook	soot
cookies	look	stood
crook	moor	took
foot	nook	wool

-UE-(blue)

accrue	due	gruel
blue	duel	hue
clue	ensue	rue
cruel	fuel	sue
cue	glue	true

DIPHTHONGS

-AU-

applause	cause	jaunt	
auction	caustic	laud	
audience	caution	launch	
audit	clause	launder	
audition	daub	laundry	
aught	daughter	laurel	
augment	daunt	maul	
august	exhaust	naughty	
auk	fault	nausea	
austere	faun	pauper	
authentic	flaunt	paunch	
author	fraud	pause	
auto	fraught	sauce	
autograph	gaudy	saunter	
autumn	gaunt	taught	
bauble	gauze	taunt	
because	haughty	taut	
caucus	haul	vault	
caught	haunch		
caulk	haunt		

-AW-

awe	lawn
awesome	lawyer
awning	mohawk
bawl	paw
brawl	pawl
brawn	pawn
caw	prawn
claw	raw
craw	saw
crawl	scrawl
dawn	shawl
draw	slaw
drawl	spawn
drawn	sprawl
fawn	squaw
flaw	straw
gnaw	thaw
hawk	trawl
hawthorn	withdraw
jaw	yawn
law	

-EW-

anew	dew	mew	slew
askew	drew	new	spew
bedew	flew	newt	stew
blew	grew	pew	strew
brew	hew	renew	threw
chew	jewel	review	view
clew	knew	shrew	yew
crew	lewd	skew	

-OI-

adjoin	despoil	loin	rejoice
anoint	devoid	moil	rejoin
appoint	disappoint	moist	roil
asteroid	disjointed	noise	soil
avoid	embroil	oil	spoil
boil	enjoin	ointment	subjoin
broil	foil	point	toil
choice	foist	poise	turmoil
coil	hoist	purloin	voice
coin	join	quoin	void
conjoint	joint	quoit	
counterpoint	joist	recoil	

15

-OU-

abound
about
account
aground
aloud
amount
announce
astound
avouch
becloud
blouse
bough
bounce
bound
bout
cloud
clout
compound
confound
couch
count
crouch
denounce

devour
devout
discount
doubt
douse
enshroud
expound
flounce
flounder
flour
flout
foul
found
fount
gout
grouch
ground
grouse
grout
hound
house
impound
joust

loud
louse
lout
mound
mouse
mouth
noun
ouch
ounce
our
out
paramount
pouch
pound
pout
profound
pronounce
rebound
remount
renounce
resound
round
route

scour
scout
shout
shroud
slouch
sound
sour
south
spout
sprout
stout
surmount
surround
thou
tout
trounce
trout
vouch
without
wound

-OW-

allow
bow
bower
brow
brown
chow
chowder
clown
cow
cower
cowl
crowd
crown
down
drown
endow
flower
fowl
frown
glower
gown
growl

how
howitzer
howl
jowl
now
owl
plow
pow
powder
power
prow
prowl
renown
row
scow
shower
sow
town
vow
wow
yowl

-OY-

annoy
boy
cloy
convoy
coy
decoy
deploy
destroy
employ
enjoy
gargoyle
joy
loyal
ploy
royal
toy
troy

R-CONTROLLED WORDS

-AR-

afar	carnation	far	march	shark
arc	carp	farm	mark	sharp
are	carpet	gar	market	smart
ark	cart	garb	mart	spar
arm	carton	garment	par	spark
art	cartoon	guard	parcel	star
bar	carve	hard	parch	starch
barb	char	hark	pardon	stark
bard	charcoal	harm	park	start
bargain	charge	harmony	part	tar
barge	charm	harp	partridge	tart
bark	chart	jar	party	tsar
barn	dark	lard	radar	yard
car	darn	large	sardine	yarn
card	dart	lark	scar	
cardinal	depart	mar	scarf	

-ER-

after	jerk	perfect	pert	stern
berth	jersey	perform	pertinent	summer
clerk	merchant	perfume	reverse	supper
cover	mercury	perhaps	rubber	swerve
enter	mercy	perjury	runner	teacher
farmer	mermaid	perk	serf	term
fern	miserable	permanent	serge	terminal
germ	nerve	permission	sermon	termite
hammer	offer	permit	serpent	tern
her	percale	perplex	servant	terrain
herb	percent	persist	serve	verse
herd	perception	person	service	winter
hermit	perch	perspire	silver	wonder
hunter	percussion	persuade	sitter	

-IR-

affirm	dirt	girt	skirt	thirst
birch	fir	girth	smirch	thirty
bird	firm	irk	smirk	twirl
birth	first	mirth	squirrel	whir
chirp	firth	quirk	squirt	whirl
circle	flirt	shirk	stir	
circus	gird	shirt	swirl	
dirk	girl	sir	third	

-OR-

abhor	for	normal	sport
abort	ford	north	store
absorb	forge	or	stork
accord	fork	orb	storm
adorn	form	porch	sword
assort	forth	pork	thorn
bore	glory	port	torch
born	gorge	record	tore
chord	horn	report	torn
chore	horse	score	tornado
consort	ignore	scorn	tort
cord	important	shore	worn
core	lord	short	
cork	lorn	snore	
corn	morn	sore	
distort	nor	sort	

-UR-

blur	cursive	purge	surround
blurt	curt	purl	surtax
burden	curtain	purple	survey
burdock	curtsy	purpose	survive
burg	curve	purr	turban
burglar	fur	purse	turbine
burlap	furl	return	turbulent
burn	furnish	slur	turf
burnt	furniture	spur	turkey
burr	furrow	spurn	turmoil
burro	further	spurt	turn
burrow	hurdle	surf	turnip
burst	hurl	surface	turpentine
church	hurricane	surge	turquoise
churn	hurry	surgeon	turret
cur	hurt	surmise	turtle
curb	hurtle	surname	urban
curd	lurch	surpass	urchin
curfew	lurk	surplus	urge
curl	nurse	surprise	urgent
current	nursery	surrender	urn
curse	nurture	surrey	

INITIAL CONSONANT BLENDS

BL-

blab	blaze	blimp	blob	blotter
black	blazer	blind	block	blouse
bladder	bleach	blinder	blockade	blow
blade	bleacher	blindfold	bloke	blower
blame	bleak	blink	blond	blubber
blanch	bleary	blintz	blood	blue
bland	bleat	blip	bloodhound	blueprint
blank	bleed	bliss	bloodshed	bluff
blanket	blemish	blister	bloody	blunder
blare	blend	blithe	bloom	blunt
blarney	blender	blithering	blooper	blur
blast	bless	blitz	blossom	blurb
blat	blew	blizzard	blot	blurt
blatant	blight	bloat	blotch	blush

BR-

brace	brat	breeze	brisk	brook
bracelet	brave	brevity	bristle	broom
bracken	brawl	brew	britches	broth
bracket	brawn	briar	brittle	brother
brad	bray	brick	broach	brought
brag	brazen	bride	broad	brow
braid	brazier	bridge	brocade	brown
braille	breach	bridle	broccoli	brownie
brain	breadth	brief	brochure	browse
braise	break	brier	brogue	bruin
brake	breakfast	brig	broil	bruise
bramble	breast	brigade	broiler	brunch
bran	breath	brigand	broke	brunt
branch	breathe	bright	broken	brush
brand	bred	brilliant	broker	brusque
brandish	breech	brim	bronco	brutal
brandy	breeches	brine	bronze	brute
brash	breed	brink	brood	

CL-

clack	clarinet	clef	clinic	clot
clad	clarity	cleft	clink	cloth
claim	clash	clemency	clip	clothe
clam	clasp	clench	clipper	clothes
clamber	class	clergy	clique	cloud
clammy	classic	clerical	cloak	clout
clamor	classify	clerk	clobber	clove
clamp	clatter	clever	clock	clover
clan	clause	click	clod	clown
clang	claw	client	clog	club
clank	clay	cliff	cloister	cluck
clap	clean	climate	clone	clue
clapboard	cleanser	climax	clop	clump
clapper	clear	climb	close	clumsy
claptrap	cleat	clinch	closet	cluster
clarify	cleave	cling	closure	clutch

CR-

crab	cravat	creepy	crisp	crow
crack	crave	cremate	critic	crowd
crackel	craw	crepe	critical	crown
cracker	crawl	crept	criticize	crucial
cradle	crayfish	crescent	critter	crucify
craft	crayon	cress	croak	crud
crafty	craze	crest	crochet	crude
crag	crazy	crevasse	crock	cruel
cram	creak	crevice	crocodile	cruet
cramp	cream	crew	crocus	cruise
cranberry	crease	crib	crone	crumb
crane	create	crick	crony	crumble
cranial	creation	cricket	crook	crumpet
crank	creator	crier	crooked	crumple
cranky	creature	crime	croon	crunch
cranny	credit	crimp	crop	crusade
crappie	creed	crimson	croquet	crutch
crash	creek	cringe	cross	crux
crass	creel	crinkle	crouch	cry
crate	creep	cripple	croup	crypt

DR-

drab	drape	dregs	drivel	drowsy
dracma	drastic	drench	driver	drub
draft	drat	dress	drizzle	drudge
draftsman	draw	dresser	droll	drug
drafty	drawer	dressing	dromedary	druid
drag	drawl	drew	drone	drum
dragon	drawn	dribble	drool	drunk
drain	dray	drier	droop	dry
drake	dread	drift	dropper	dryad
dram	dream	drill	drought	dryly
drama	dreamer	drink	drove	
dramatic	dreary	drip	drown	
drank	dredge	drive	drowse	

FL-

flabbergast	flask	flew	floe	flown
flabby	flat	flex	flog	fluctuate
flag	flatten	flexible	flood	flue
flagon	flatter	flick	floor	fluent
flagrant	flaunt	flier	floozy	fluff
flail	flavor	flight	flop	fluid
flair	flaw	flimsy	floral	fluke
flake	flax	flinch	florist	flume
flame	flay	fling	floss	flunk
flamingo	flea	flint	flounce	fluorescent
flammable	fleck	flip	flounder	fluoride
flank	fledgling	flippant	flour	flurry
flannel	flee	flirt	flourish	flush
flap	fleece	flit	flout	flute
flare	fleet	float	flow	flutter
flash	flesh	flock	flower	flux

FR-

fracas	frantic	freight	frill	front
fraction	fraternal	frenzy	fringe	frontier
fracture	fraud	frequent	frisk	frost
fragile	fraught	fresh	fritter	frosty
fragment	fray	fret	frivolous	froth
fragrance	frazzle	friar	frizz	frown
fragrant	freak	friction	frizzle	frozen
frail	freckle	fried	frock	frugal
frame	free	friend	frog	fruit
franc	freedom	frigate	frolic	frustrate
franchise	freeze	fright	from	fry
frank	freezer	frigid	frond	

GL-

glacial	gland	glib	gloat	glove
glacier	glare	glide	glob	glow
glad	glass	glider	globe	glucose
glade	glaze	glimmer	gloom	glue
gladiator	gleam	glimpse	glorious	glum
gladly	glean	glint	glory	glut
glamour	glee	glisten	gloss	glycerin
glance	glen	glitter	glossary	

GR-

grab	graph	great	grin	gross
grace	graphic	greatly	grind	grouch
gracious	grapple	greed	grinder	ground
grade	grasp	green	grip	group
gradual	grass	greet	gripe	grouse
graduate	grate	grenade	grisly	grove
graduation	grateful	grew	gristle	grovel
graft	gratify	grey	grit	grow
grain	gratis	grid	gritty	growl
gram	gratitude	griddle	grizzly	grown
grammar	grave	grief	groan	growth
granary	gravel	grievance	grocer	grudge
grand	gravity	grieve	grog	gruel
granite	gravy	griffin	groggy	gruff
grant	gray	grill	groin	grumble
granular	graze	grim	groom	grumpy
grape	grease	grime	groove	grunt
grapefruit	greasy	grimy	grope	

PL-

placard	planter	plead	pluck
placate	plaque	pleasant	plug
place	plasma	please	plum
placement	plaster	pleasure	plumage
placid	plastic	pleat	plumb
plaid	plate	pledge	plumber
plain	plateau	plentiful	plume
plaint	platform	plenty	plummet
plaintiff	platinum	pliable	plump
plait	platoon	pliant	plunder
plan	platter	pliers	plunge
plane	platypus	plight	plunger
planet	plausible	plod	plunk
plank	play	plop	plural
plankton	player	plot	plus
planner	plaza	plow	plush
plant	plea	ploy	ply

PR-

practical	prestige	privilege	promise
practice	pretend	prize	promote
prairie	pretty	probable	prompt
praise	preview	probably	prone
prance	prey	probe	prong
prank	price	problem	pronounce
prattle	prick	proceed	proof
prawn	prickle	process	prop
pray	pride	procession	propel
prayer	priest	proclaim	proper
preach	prim	produce	property
precinct	prime	profess	propose
precious	primitive	profession	prose
precise	primp	professor	protect
predict	prince	profile	protest
prefer	princess	profit	proud
premise	principal	profound	prove
prepare	print	profuse	prow
present	prior	program	prowl
preserve	prism	progress	prude
president	prison	prohibit	prudent
press	private	project	prune
pressure			

SCH-
schedule
scheme
scholar
scholarship
scholastic
school
schooner

SCR-
scrag
scrap
scrape
scratch
scrawl
scrawny
scream
screech
screen
screw
scribble
scribe
scrim
scrimmage
scrimp
script
scrub
scruple
scrutiny

SHR-
shrank
shrapnel
shred
shrew
shrewd
shriek
shrift
shrike
shrill
shrimp
shrine
shrink
shrive
shrivel
shroud
shrub
shrug
shrunk

SK-
skate
skeleton
skeptic
sketch
skew
skewer
ski
skid
skiff
skill
skim
skimp
skin
skip
skirmish
skirt
skit
skulk
skull
skunk
sky

SL-
slab
slack
slacks
slag
slain
slake
slalom
slam
slander
slang
slant
slap
slapstick
slash
slat
slate
slaughter
slave
slavery

slaw
slay
sleazy
sled
sledge
sleek
sleep
sleepy
sleet
sleeve
sleigh
sleight
slender
slept
sleuth
slew
slice
slicer
slick

slicker
slid
slide
slight
slim
slime
sling
slink
slip
slipper
slit
slither
sliver
slob
slobber
slogan
sloop
slop
slope

sloppy
slosh
slot
sloth
slouch
slovenly
slow
sludge
slug
slugger
sluice
slum
slumber
slump
slung
slunk
slur
slurp
slush
sly

SM-

smack	smile	smock	smother
smart	smirch	smog	smudge
smash	smirk	smoke	smug
smear	smite	smolder	smuggle
smell	smith	smooth	smut
smelt	smitten	smote	

SN-

snack	sneak	snipe	snout
snail	sneer	snivel	snow
snake	sneeze	snob	snub
snap	snicker	snoop	snuff
snare	sniff	snooze	snuffle
snarl	sniffle	snore	snug
snatch	snip	snort	snuggle

SP-

spa	special	spinet	spud
space	species	spire	spume
spade	specific	spirit	spunk
span	speck	spit	spur
spangle	speckle	spite	spurt
spank	sped	spittle	sputter
spar	speech	splice	spy
spare	speed	split	
spark	spell	spoil	
sparkle	spend	spoke	
sparrow	spent	sponge	
sparse	spew	spool	
spasm	spider	spoon	
spat	spike	spoor	
spatter	spill	sport	
spawn	spin	spot	
speak	spindle	spouse	
spear	spine	spout	

SPL-

splash	spleen	splice	splotch
splatter	splendid	splint	splurge
splay	splendor	split	splutter

SPR-

sprain	spray	spring	sprout
sprang	spread	sprinkle	spruce
sprat	spree	sprint	sprung
sprawl	sprig	sprit	spry

SQU-

squab	squander	squeak	squib
squabble	square	squeal	squid
squad	squash	squeamish	squint
squalid	squat	squeeze	squire
squall	squaw	squelch	squirm
squalor			squirt

ST-

stab	start	step	stork
stable	starve	sterile	storm
stack	stash	stern	story
stadium	state	stew	stout
staff	static	stick	stove
stag	status	stiff	stow
stage	staunch	stifle	stub
stagger	stave	still	stubble
stagnant	stay	stilt	stud
staid	stead	sting	student
stain	steady	stink	stuff
stair	steal	stint	stumble
stake	stealth	stir	stump
stale	steam	stitch	stun
stalk	steed	stock	stung
stall	steel	stole	stunt
stamp	steep	stone	stupid
stand	steeple	stood	sturdy
staple	steer	stop	sty
star	stein	store	style
stark			

STR-

straddle	straw	strew	stroke
strafe	stray	strict	stroll
straight	streak	stride	strong
strain	stream	strife	strove
strait	street	strike	struggle
strand	strength	string	strut
strangle	stress	strip	
strap	stretch		

SW-

swab	swat	swept	swirl
swag	swath	swift	swish
swain	sway	swig	switch
swallow	swear	swill	swivel
swam	sweat	swim	swoop
swamp	sweep	swindle	sworn
swan	sweet	swine	
swap	swell	swing	
swarm	swelter	swipe	

TR-

trace	trapper	tribute	trooper
track	trash	trick	trophy
tract	trashy	trickle	tropic
traction	travel	tricky	tropical
tractor	traverse	tried	trot
trade	trawl	trifle	trouble
tradition	trawler	trigger	trough
traffic	tray	trillion	trounce
tragedy	tread	trim	trout
tragic	treason	trio	truce
trail	treat	trip	truck
trailer	treaty	tripe	trudge
train	tree	triple	true
trainer	trek	tripod	truly
trait	tremble	trite	trump
traitor	tremor	triumph	trumpet
tramp	trench	trivet	trundle
trample	trend	trivia	trunk
trance	trespass	trivial	truss
transfer	tress	trod	trust
transit	trestle	troll	trusty
transmit	trial	trolley	truth
trap	triangle	trombone	try
trapeze	tribe	troop	tryst

TW-

twang	twentieth	twin	twist
tweak	twenty	twine	twit
tweed	twice	twinge	twitch
tweezers	twiddle	twinkle	twitter
twelfth	twig	twinkling	
twelve	twilight	twirl	

FINAL CONSONANT BLENDS

-DGE

abridge	dodge	grudge	misjudge	sludge
adjudge	dredge	hedge	nudge	smudge
badge	drudge	judge	pledge	trudge
bridge	edge	kedge	ridge	wedge
budge	fledge	ledge	sedge	
cadge	fudge	lodge	sledge	

-FT

			-LK	
adrift	gift	shift	bilk	milk
aft	graft	soft	bulk	silk
aloft	haft	swift	elk	sulk
cleft	left	theft	hulk	walk
craft	lift	thrift		
daft	loft	tuft		
deft	oft	waft		
draft	raft	weft		
drift	rift			

-NT

absent	event	hint	pint	sent
anoint	extent	hunt	plant	shunt
ant	faint	indent	point	slant
appoint	flaunt	invent	print	spent
aunt	flint	jaunt	punt	sprint
bent	footprint	joint	quaint	squint
blunt	fount	lent	rant	stint
brunt	front	lint	rent	stunt
bunt	gent	mint	resent	taunt
cent	glint	mount	runt	tent
chant	grant	paint	saint	tint
dent	grunt	pant	scant	vent
dint	haunt	pent	scent	want
				went

-ND

abscond	bond	gland	mound	spend
and	bound	grand	pond	stand
around	brand	grind	pound	strand
band	command	ground	rand	tend
behind	end	hand	refund	trend
bend	fend	hind	remind	vend
beyond	find	hound	rend	wand
bind	fond	kind	rind	wind
bland	found	land	rotund	withstand
blend	friend	lend	round	wound
blind	frond	mend	send	
blond	fund	mind	sound	

-NG

bang, bing, bong, bring, clang, cling, clung, ding, dong, dung, fang, fling, gang, gong, hang, hung, king, long, lung, pang, ping, pong, prong, rang, rung, sang, sing, slang, sling, sprang, spring, sting, stung, sung, swing, ting, wing, wrong, zing

-NK

bank, blank, blink, bonk, brink, bunk, clank, clunk, crank, dank, drank, drink, drunk, dunk, fink, flank, frank, hank, honk, junk, kink, lank, link, mink, pink, plink, plunk, prank, rank, rink, sank, shank, sink, slink, spank, spunk, stank, stink, stunk, sunk, swank, tank, wink

-PT

abrupt, accept, adapt, adept, adopt, apt, corrupt, crept, disrupt, erupt, except, inept, interrupt, kept, opt, prompt, rapt, sept, slept, swept, wept, wrapt

-SP

asp, clasp, crisp, gasp, grasp, hasp, lisp, rasp, wasp, wisp

-ST

aghast, beast, best, blast, blest, boast, breast, bust, cast, chest, coast, cost, crest, crust, cyst, disgust, dust, east, exist, fast, feast, fest, fist, frost, ghost, gist, grist, guest, gust, hoist, host, jest, last, least, lest, list, lost, mast, mist, most, must, nest, past, pest, post, priest, quest, rest, roast, rust, test, thirst, toast, trust, tryst, vast, vest, west, wrest, wrist, yeast, zest

INITIAL CONSONANT DIGRAPHS

CH-

chafe	chapter	cheese	chip
chain	charcoal	cherry	chipmunk
chair	charge	chess	chirp
chaise	chariot	chest	chive
chalk	charm	chew	chocolate
challenge	charming	chick	choice
chamber	chase	chicken	choke
champ	chat	chief	chop
champion	chatter	child	chubby
chance	cheap	chill	chuck
change	cheat	chilly	chum
channel	check	chime	chunk
chant	checker	chimney	church
chap	cheek	chin	churn
chapel	cheer	china	

KN-

		PH-	
knack	knit	phalanx	phoebe
knapsack	knob	phantasm	phoenix
knave	knock	phantom	phone
knead	knoll	pharmacist	phonics
knee	knot	pharmacy	phonograph
kneel	know	pharynx	phony
knell	knowledge	phase	phosphate
knelt	known	pheasant	photo
knew	knuckle	phenomenal	photograph
knickknack		philanthropy	phrase
knife		philosopher	physic
knight		philosophy	physical
		phlegm	physician
		phlegmatic	physics
		phlox	physiology
		phobia	physique

QU-

		SH-	
quack	query	shadow	shine
quaff	quest	shake	ship
quail	question	shallow	shirt
quaint	quibble	shame	shock
quake	quick	shampoo	shoe
qualm	quiet	shape	shoot
quarry	quill	shark	shop
quart	quilt	sharp	short
quartz	quince	shed	should
quaver	quip	sheet	
quay	quirk	shell	
queasy	quite		
queen	quiver		
queer	quiz		
quell	quota		
quench	quote		

TH-(then)

than	they		
that	thine		
the	this		
thee	those		
their	thou		
them	though		
themselves	thus		
then	thy		
thence			
there			
these			

TH-(thin)

thank	thirst
thankful	thirsty
thatch	thirty
theater	thistle
theft	thong
theme	thorn
thermal	thorny
thermometer	thorough
thesis	thought
thick	thousand
thief	thud
thigh	thug
thimble	thumb
thin	thump
think	thunder
third	

WH-

whack	whimsical
whale	whine
wharf	whinny
what	whip
wheat	whir
wheedle	whirl
wheel	whisk
wheeze	whisker
whelp	whisper
when	whist
whence	whistle
where	white
whether	whither
whey	whittle
which	whoa
whiff	whopper
while	whorl
whim	why

WR-

wrack	wright
wraith	wring
wrangle	wrinkle
wrap	wrist
wrath	writ
wreak	write
wreath	writhe
wreck	wrong
wren	wrote
wrench	wrought
wrest	wrung
wrestle	wry
wretch	
wriggle	

MEDIAL AND FINAL CONSONANT DIGRAPHS

PH-(medial and final)

alphabet	elephant	nymph	trophy
autograph	gopher	orphan	typhoid
dolphin	nephew	triumph	typhoon

-CH (final)

arch	brunch	ditch	leech	preach	switch
attach	bunch	drench	lunch	punch	teach
batch	catch	each	march	reach	thatch
beach	church	fetch	match	scratch	touch
beech	cinch	finch	much	screech	twitch
bench	clench	fletch	munch	search	vetch
beseech	clinch	flinch	notch	sketch	watch
birch	clutch	hatch	parch	snatch	wench
bitch	coach	hitch	patch	speech	which
bleach	couch	hutch	peach	splotch	witch
blotch	crotch	graph	perch	starch	wrench
botch	crunch	impeach	pinch	stich	wretch
breach	crutch	inch	pitch	stretch	
breech	detach	itch	poach		
broach	dispatch	latch			

-CK (final)

back	fleck	pack	snack		
black	flick	peck	sock		
block	flock	pick	speck		
brick	frock	pluck	stack		
buck	hack	pock	stick		
check	hick	prick	stock		
chick	hock	puck	struck		
chuck	jack	quack	stuck		
clack	kick	quick	suck		
click	knack	rack	tack		
clock	knock	rock	thick		
cluck	lack	sack	tick		
cock	lick	shack	track		
crack	lock	shock	treck		
crick	luck	shuck	trick		
crock	mock	sick	truck		
deck	muck	slack	tuck		
dock	neck	smack	whack		
duck	nick	smock	wick		

-GH (final)

cough
enough
laugh
rough
tough
trough

-LK (final)

balk
bilk
bulk
calk
caulk
chalk
elk
folk
hulk
milk
silk
stalk
sulk
walk
whelk

-SH (final)

abash	flesh	rash			
afresh	flush	rush			
ash	fresh	sash			
bash	gash	shush			
blush	gnash	slash			
brash	gush	slosh			
brush	hash	slush			
bush	hush	smash			
cash	lash	splash			
clash	lush	squash			
crash	mash	squish			
crush	mesh	stash			
dash	mush	swish			
dish	plush	thrash			
enmesh	posh	thresh			
fish	push	thrush			

-TH (final)

aftermath	hath	quoth
bath	health	sheath
beneath	heath	sixth
birth	herewith	sloth
both	lath	smith
breath	length	south
broth	loth	strength
cloth	math	teeth
death	mirth	troth
depth	month	wealth
fifth	moth	width
filth	mouth	with
forth	ninth	wrath
froth	oath	wreath
girth	path	
growth	pith	

VARIANT CONSONANT SOUNDS

Hard C

cab	canary	carol	coat	come	country
cabbage	cancel	carpet	cob	comment	coupon
cabin	candle	carrot	cobweb	common	court
cable	candy	carry	cock	company	cover
caboose	cane	cart	cocoa	compass	cow
cactus	cannon	carton	cod	concern	cozy
cage	canoe	carve	code	cone	cub
cake	canteen	case	coffee	conflict	cube
calculate	canyon	cat	coil	contain	cuff
calendar	cape	catalog	coin	contest	culture
calf	capital	catch	cold	control	curse
calm	capsule	caterpillar	collar	cook	custom
calorie	capture	caution	collect	copy	cut
came	car	cave	colony	cork	cute
camel	carbon	caw	color	corn	
camp	card	coach	colt	correct	
campus	care	coal	column	cost	
can	carnival	coast	comb	cottage	

Soft C

cedar	cinch
ceiling	cinder
celery	cinnamon
cell	circle
cellar	cite
cement	citizen
cent	citrus
center	city
central	civil
cereal	civilization
ceremony	cycle
certain	cyclone
cider	cylinder
cigar	cymbal
cigarette	cypress
	cyst

Hard G

gab	garage	go	gray
gable	garden	goal	green
gadget	gargle	goat	grin
gage	garland	gobble	groan
gain	garlic	goggles	ground
gait	garment	gold	guarantee
galaxy	gas	golf	guard
gale	gash	gone	guess
gall	gasoline	good	guest
gallant	gate	goose	guide
gallery	gather	gopher	guilt
gallon	gauge	gorilla	guitar
gallop	gauze	gossip	gulf
galore	gave	got	gull
galoshes	gay	government	gum
gamble	gaze	gown	gun
game	glad	grade	guppy
gang	globe	grape	gutter
gape	glove	grass	guy

Soft G

gelatin	gesture
gem	giant
general	ginger
generation	giraffe
generous	gym
gentle	gymnasium
genuine	gyp
geography	gypsy
geometry	gyrate
germ	gyroscope

-GHT Letter Group

blight	flight	might	slight
bought	fought	night	sought
bright	fraught	nought	thought
brought	fright	ought	tight
caught	height	plight	weight
eight	knight	right	wright
fight	light	sight	wrought

RHYMING PAIRS

These are word pairs that can be used for vocabulary development. The pairs (usually an adjective and a noun) rhyme and present humorous word pictures. These pairs are sometimes called "Hink Pinks."

To introduce this activity to students, the teacher might ask, "What is a Hink Pink for _____ _____ ?" (giving the definitions), and then wait for students to supply the rhyming pair.

Example: What is a Hink Pink for an overweight feline?
Hink Pink Answer: A fat cat.

The teacher might also ask students to provide the definition of a given Hink Pink.

Example: What is the definition of a sad dad?
Answer: An unhappy father.

A "Hink Pink" is used to denote pairs of one syllable each.
A "Hinky Pinky" is used to denote pairs of two syllables each.
A "Hinkety Pinkety" is used to denote pairs of three syllables each.

Pair	Definition
drab cab	a dreary taxi
race pace	a rate of speed in a running event
black crack	a dark crevice
glad lad	a happy boy
bear scare	a fright caused by a grizzly
rag bag	a sack for cloth scraps
frail male	a weak man
pale whale	a pallid sea mammal
brain strain	cerebral overwork
fake snake	a fradulent reptile
chalk talk	a blackboard discussion
sham ram	a fake male sheep
damp camp	a wet campground
chance glance	a lucky gimpse
clap trap	a trick to win applause
grim hymn	a stern church song
limp blimp	a dirigible with no air
fine pine	excellent grade spruce tree
pink drink	a light red beverage
bright light	brilliant illumination
brighter writer	a smarter author
wise prize	an intelligent award
dock lock	a key-operated fastening to secure a pier
cold gold	a cool, yellow precious metal
stone bone	a petrified femur
long song	a lengthy tune
rude dude	a crude guy
book crook	a manuscript thief
broom room	a closet for storing a sweeping tool
loose noose	a hangman's knot that is not tight

Pair	Definition
harsh marsh	a rough and unpleasant swamp
smart start	an intelligent beginning
last blast	the final explosion
great date	a wonderful appointment
bath path	a trail to the shower
fraud abroad	trickery overseas
brave slave	a courageous servant
fall brawl	an autumn fight
wax tax	a levy on polish
clay tray	a carrying device made of an earthen material
beach speach	a talk at the seashore
weak Greek	a feeble man from Greece
steel wheel	an iron steering device
dream scream	a nightmarish cry or yell
beast feast	a monster's banquet
sweet treat	a sugary feast
deck check	a ship's flooring inspection
red shed	a crimson shack
free bee	a honey-making insect that doesn't cost anything
cheap sheep	an inexpensive lamb
hen pen	a cage for chickens
bent cent	a crooked penny
tent rent	money paid for canvas lodging
terse verse	a concise rhyme
wet pet	a damp domestic animal
blue hue	an aqua shade
tribe scribe	the note taker for an Indian group
nice price	a fair cost
crop flop	failure of a farm's produce
rope soap	detergent for cleaning heavy line
floor store	a shop where flooring is purchased
pork fork	a utensil used to eat pig meat
cross boss	an angry employer
host boast	a party giver's bragging
loud crowd	a noisy group
sound hound	a healthy dog
flower shower	a rain of posies
mouse house	a dwelling for mice
stout scout	a fat person who is sent out to look ahead
low blow	a punch below the waist
slow crow	a black bird that does not fly quickly
brown crown	a tan headpiece for a ruling person
duck truck	a vehicle for transporting waterfowl
mud flood	an inundation of water and dirt
fudge judge	a person who must choose the best chocolate candy
glum chum	a sad or unhappy friend
fun run	an enjoyable jog
tall wall	a high stone fence
skunk bunk	a bed for a smelly mammal
time chime	an hour bell
pig wig	a hog's hairpiece
funny bunny	a humorous rabbit
pure cure	untainted medicine
mute lute	a soundless, pear-shaped stringed instrument
cute newt	an attractive land salamander
quick pick	a rapid selection
dry fly	a bothersome insect that is not wet

OPEN AND CLOSED SYLLABLE WORDS

V-CV/Open Syllable Words

agent	decide	futile	minus	silence
baby	defeat	genius	miser	siphon
bacon	defend	glacier	moment	sober
baker	dilate	gopher	motel	soda
basis	diner	gyrate	nature	solo
before	eject	haven	navy	spiral
below	elect	hero	omit	spoken
blatant	erase	hobo	open	tiger
bonus	evade	hotel	oval	vacant
cedar	even	ibex	pilot	vapor
chosen	evil	ibis	polo	veto
cider	fatal	icy	quaver	vocal
climate	favor	label	radar	wager
clover	fever	labor	razor	yodel
cocoa	fiber	lady	recent	zebra
cohort	final	local	recess	zero
cycle	flavor	locate	require	
decay	frozen	major		

VC-CV/Closed Syllable Words

admit	fifteen	lancer	plastic	tennis
appoint	foggy	letter	problem	tractor
ballad	follow	lumber	public	traffic
bamboo	ginger	master	quagmire	trigger
bandit	goblin	member	question	tunnel
better	gossip	metric	quitter	ulcer
bonnet	hobby	motto	rascal	umpire
cactus	hollow	muffin	rescue	under
candy	ignite	napkin	robber	upper
cotton	imbed	nectar	rubber	vampire
daddy	index	number	silver	velvet
dentist	issue	nutmeg	splendid	victor
disgust	jelly	object	splinter	welcome
doctor	jobber	offer	suffer	western
dummy	justice	optic	summer	whisper
effort	kennel	picnic	supper	window
endure	kitten	pillow	tamper	yellow
fancy	ladder	pistol	temper	yonder
				zipper

-LE Words/Closed Syllable

amble	dibble	knuckle	riddle	stumble
ample	dimple	little	ripple	subtle
angle	dingle	mangle	rubble	suckle
ankle	dribble	mantle	ruffle	supple
apple	drizzle	meddle	rumble	tackle
babble	dwindle	middle	rumple	tangle
baffle	fickle	mingle	saddle	tattle
bangle	fiddle	mottle	sample	temple
battle	fizzle	muddle	scribble	thimble
bobble	fondle	muffle	scuffle	thistle
bottle	frazzle	mumble	scuttle	throttle
bramble	freckle	muscle	settle	tickle
brindle	frizzle	muzzle	shackle	tingle
bristle	fumble	nestle	shingle	tipple
brittle	gamble	nettle	shuffle	topple
bubble	gentle	nibble	shuttle	trample
buckle	giggle	niggle	sickle	tremble
bundle	gobble	nimble	simple	trestle
bungle	grapple	nipple	single	trickle
bustle	griddle	nozzle	sizzle	truckle
cackle	grumble	nuzzle	smuggle	truffle
candle	haggle	paddle	snaffle	trundle
castle	handle	pebble	sniffle	tumble
cattle	heckle	pestle	snuffle	twiddle
chuckle	huddle	pickle	snuggle	twinkle
cobble	humble	piddle	spangle	uncle
cockle	hustle	pimple	sparkle	wabble
coddle	jangle	prattle	spindle	waddle
crackle	jiggle	prickle	spittle	waffle
cripple	jingle	puddle	sprinkle	waggle
crumble	joggle	puzzle	squiggle	whittle
crumple	jostle	quibble	stickle	wiggle
cuddle	juggle	rabble	straddle	wimple
dabble	jumble	raffle	straggle	wrangle
dangle	jungle	ramble	strangle	wrestle
dapple	kettle	rankle	struggle	wrinkle
dazzle	kindle	rattle	stubble	wriggle

-LE Words/Open Syllable

able	cable	gable	sable	stifle
beadle	cradle	idle	scruple	table
beagle	cycle	ladle	sidle	title
beetle	eagle	maple	stable	treacle
bridle	fable	people	staple	trifle
bugle	feeble	rifle	steeple	wheedle

PREFIXES

a-, ab (away from)

abide
abloom
abnormal
abode
abound

ante- (before)

antecede
antechamber
antenatal
antepenult
anteroom
antetype

anti- (against)

antibacterial
antibody
anticatalyst
anticlerical
antifreeze
antitank
antitoxin
antiwar

auto- (self)

autobiography
autobus
autoharp
autohypnosis
automobile

bi- (two)

bicycle
bimetal
bimonthly
bipolar
biweekly

circum- (around)

circumnavigate
circumpolar
circumscribe

co- (together, with)

cobelligerents
coefficient
coexist
cohabit
coheir

counter-(against)

counteract
counterattack
counterbalance
counterclaim
counterculture
counterrevolution
counterspy
counterweight

de- (away, down)

deactivate
debar
debase
debrief
decamp
degrade
dehumidify
delouse

dis- (apart from, not)

disallow
disappoint
disarm
discontinue
discount
discredit
disenchant
dislocate
disobey

ex- (from)

excogitate
excommunicate
exfoliate
exterminate

extra- (outside, beyond)

extracurricular
extragalactic
extrajudicial
extralegal
extraordinary
extrasensory
extraterritorial

fore- (in front)

forearm
forebode
forecastle
forefinger
forefoot
forefront
foreground
forehand
forehead
foremast

il- (not)

illegal
illegible
illiterate
illogical

im- (not)

immaterial
immature
immeasurable
imperfect
impersonal
impolite
improper
impure

in- (not)

inaccessible
inactive
inarticulate
inclement
incomplete
inconvenient
independent
indifferent
indirect
insane

inter- (between, among)

interact
intercede
interchange
intercontinental
intermingle
intermix
intersection
interstellar

ir- (not)

irradiate
irrational
irregular
irrelevant
irreligious
irreplaceable
irrepressible
irresponsible
irreverent
irreversible

mid- (middle)

midair
midday
midland
midnight
midpoint
midships
midsummer

mis- (wrong)

misadventure
misapply
miscast
miscue
misfortune
misname
misspell
misstep
misunderstand

non- (not)

nonabrasive
nonburnable
nonconductor
nondurable
nonentity
nonsmoker
nonviolent
nonvocal
nonvoter
nonunion

over- (over)

overactive
overbold
overcharge
overdress
overgrown
overlay
overplay
overreact
overrun
overtax

post- (after)

postdate
postoperative
postscript
postwar

pre- (before)

precaution
preclude
precursor
predate
predict
prefabricate
prefix
premarital
prepay
presume

pro-(before, in front, forward, forth)

procreate
produce
profess
profile
profound
project
pronoun
provoke

re- (again)

reclaim
redo
refinish
reline
relive
remount
repaint
replace

sub- (under)

subdivide
submarine
subnormal
subplot
subsoil
substandard
suburban

super- (over)

supercede
supercharge
superego
superhighway
superhuman
superman
supermarket
supernatural
supernova

tele- (far away)

telegram
telegraph
telephone
telephoto
telescope
television

trans- (across)

translucent
transmigrate
transplant
transpolar
transport
transpose

un- (not)

unclear
uneven
unfair
unfit
unglue
unhook
unlace
unlock
unpack
untie
untouched

uni- (one)

unicellular
unicycle
unilateral

SUFFIXES

-able
(tending to, able to)

conquerable
enjoyable
lovable
payable
perishable
readable
reliable
washable

-age
(state of being)
(place of, result of)

anchorage
orphanage
parsonage
personage
shrinkage
wastage

-al
(relating to)

commercial
electrical
residential
technical
theatrical

-ance, -ence
(state of being)

allowance
attendance
difference
excellence
importance

-ary, -ery
(that which, place where)

bakery
cannery
creamery
dictionary
forgery
nursery
revolutionary

-en
(having nature of)

ashen
broken
earthen
fallen
golden
molten
spoken
swollen
wooden
woven

-en
(to make or become)

blacken
fatten
flatten
lengthen
roughen
shorten
straighten
whiten
widen

-er
(one who, that which)

baker
carpenter
cleaner
foreigner
grocer
jumper
preacher
runner
teacher
worker

-er
(more "in degree")

faster
fatter
lighter
nicer
shorter
sicker
slower
smarter
stronger
taller

-est
(most "in degree")

cleanest
deepest
easiest
farthest
latest
longest
loudest
skinniest
tightest
widest

-ful
(characterized by, full of)

awful
beautiful
graceful
helpful
masterful
plentiful
skillful
successful
thankful
wonderful

-fy
(make or form into)

clarify
glorify
horrify
identify
justify
modify
notify
qualify
simplify
testify

-hood
(state of rank)

adulthood
boyhood
brotherhood
childhood
falsehood
maidenhood
manhood
neighborhood
priesthood
womanhood

-ic
(pertaining to, like)

angelic
artistic
athletic
atmospheric
classic
critic
dramatic
historic
volcanic

-ish
(having
nature of)

bluish
childish
clownish
fiendish
foolish
sickish
whitish

-ist
(one who)

artist
biologist
botanist
communist
humorist
journalist
loyalist
optomist
pessimist
pianist

-ity, -ty
(state of being)

acidity
purity
reality
sovereignty

-ive
(having nature or
(quality of, given to)

active
corrective
destructive
effective
explosive
festive
impressive
inventive
protective

-less
(without)

ageless
childless
fatherless
graceless
helpless
hopeless
merciless
penniless
priceless
witless
worthless

-ly
(in the
manner of)

actively
attentively
happily
justly
patiently
quietly
rapidly
sadly
silently
swiftly

-ment
(resulting state,
action or process)

amazement
commitment
employment
movement
payment
placement
punishment
refinement
settlement
treatment

-most
(most "in degree")

aftermost
bottommost
foremost
furthermost
hindmost
innermost
northernmost
outermost
topmost

-ness
(quality or
state of being)

blindness
gladness
goodness
kindness
likeness
sickness
sweetness
thickness
weakness
wickedness

-or
(person who,
state of quality)

actor
auditor
creditor
debtor
executor
supervisor

-ous
(state or condition,
having quality of)

courageous
dangerous
humorous
joyous
nervous
prosperous

-ship
(office, profession,
art, or skill)

championship
fellowship
friendship
hardship
horsemanship
marksmanship
partnership
penmanship
relationship
sportsmanship

-tion, -ion
(act, process,
state)

action
attraction
collection
correction
dictation
education
election
narration
protection
rejection

-ure
(act, process)

adventure
composure
enclosure
failure
pleasure

CONTRACTIONS, CONJUNCTIONS, AND PREPOSITIONS

Contractions

aren't	she'd
can't	she'll
couldn't	she's
didn't	shouldn't
doesn't	that's
don't	there's
hadn't	they'd
hasn't	they'll
haven't	they're
he'd	wasn't
he'll	we'd
here's	we'll
he's	we're
I'd	weren't
I'll	what's
I'm	where's
isn't	who'd
it's	who's
I've	won't
let's	wouldn't
mustn't	you'll
	you're
	you've

Conjunctions

Coordinating

and
but
for
nor
or
so
yet

Subordinating

after
because
if
since
till
when
where
while

Prepositions

about	inside
above	into
across	like
after	of
along	off
among	on
amongst	onto
around	out
as	outside
at	over
before	through
behind	to
below	toward
beside	under
between	underneath
by	until
down	up
for	upon
from	with
in	within

COMPOUND WORDS

afternoon	countryman	goldfish
airline	countryside	grandfather
airplane	courthouse	grandmother
alongside	courtyard	grasshopper
anybody	cowboy	grassland
anyone	craftsman	hairbrush
anyplace	crossbow	halfway
anything	daybreak	handkerchief
anytime	daytime	handshake
anyway	dishpan	handwriting
anywhere	doorbell	headdress
arrowhead	doorway	headline
backbone	downhill	highlands
backyard	downstairs	highway
baseball	downstream	hillside
baseman	downtown	homeland
basketball	driftwood	homemade
bathrobe	driveway	homework
bathroom	drugstore	hopscotch
bathtub	dugout	horseback
bedroom	earthquake	horseman
bedtime	eggshell	horseshoe
beehive	elsewhere	hourglass
birdbath	everybody	houseboat
blackboard	everyday	household
blacksmith	everyone	housewife
boathouse	everything	however
boldface	everywhere	icebox
broomstick	eyebrow	indoor
buckskin	eyelid	inland
businessmen	farewell	inside
butterfly	farmhouse	intake
campfire	farmland	into
campground	fingerprint	junkyard
candlestick	fireman	landmark
cannot	firewood	landowner
catfish	fireworks	lifetime
chairman	flagpole	lighthouse
chalkboard	flashlight	lightweight
checkerboard	flowerpot	limestone
cheeseburger	football	lookout
classmate	footprint	lowlands
classroom	footstep	mailbox
coastline	forget	mainland
coffeepot	framework	moonlight
commonplace	freshman	mountainside
corncob	furthermore	
cornfield	gingerbread	

newspaper
nightfall
nobody
northeast
northwest
notebook
nothing
nowhere
offspring
otherwise
outcome
outdoors
outline
outside
overall
overcome
overhead
overlook
overnight
paintbrush
pancake
playground
policeman
popcorn
proofread
quarterback
railroad
railway
raincoat
raindrop
rainfall
rattlesnake
roadside
rowboat
runaway
runway

sailboat
salesman
sandstone
scarecrow
schoolhouse
schoolroom
scrapbook
seaport
seashell
seashore
seaweed
sidewalk
snowball
snowflake
snowman
somebody
someday
somehow
someone
something
sometime
somewhat
somewhere
southeast
southwest
spaceship
springtime
stagecoach
stairway
starfish
steamboat
storekeeper
suitcase
summertime
sundown
sunlight
sunrise
sunset
sunshine

textbook
themselves
thereafter
throughout
townspeople
treetop
typewriter
undergo
underground
underline
underlying
underside
understand
underwater
upright
upstream
vineyard
warehouse
waterfall
waterway
weekend
whatever
whenever
whereas
wherever
whoever
widespread
wildlife
windmill
withdraw
within
without
woodland
worthwhile
yourself

SELECTED ABBREVIATIONS

A.D.	Anno Domini, in the year of our Lord		elem.	elementary
ad., adv.	advertisement		enc.	enclosure
A.M., a.m.	ante meridiem, before noon		enc.	encyclopedia
Amer.	America; American		Eng.	English
anon.	anonymous		Esq.	Esquire
apt.	apartment		E.S.T.	Eastern Standard Time
assoc.	association		etc.	et cetera, and so forth
asst.	assistant		F	Fahrenheit
atty.	attorney		FBI	Federal Bureau of Investigation
ave.	avenue		FDA	Food and Drug Administration
B.A.	Bachelor of Arts		fig.	figure
B.C.	Before Christ; British Columbia		Fr.	Father; Friar; French
bibliog.	bibliography		Fri.	Friday
bldg.	building		ft.	feet
blvd.	boulevard		gal.	gallon
bros.	brothers		geog.	geography
bur.	bureau		Gov.	Governor
C	Centigrade; Celsius		govt.	government
cal.	calories		grad.	graduate; graduated
cap.	capital		gr.	gram
cdr.	commander		hdqrs.	headquarters
cent.	century		Heb.	Hebrew; Hebrews
ch., chap.	chapter		hist.	historical; history
chm.	chairman		Hon.	Honorable
cm.	centimeter		ht.	height; heat
c/o	care of		I., i.	island
co.	company; county		ibid.	ibidem, in the same place
c.o.d.	cash on delivery collect on delivery		ill., illus.	illustration
coll.	college; collection		inc.	incorporated; including
conf.	conference		in.	inch
Cont.	Continental		incog.	incognito (unknown)
cont.	continued		Ind.	Indian
coop.	cooperative		ins.	insurance
cop., ©	copyright		int.	interest; international
corp.	corporation		intro.	introduction
C.S.T.	Central Standard Time		I.O.U.	I owe you
D.A.	District Attorney		I.Q.	intelligence quotient
DDT	dichloro-diphenyl-trichloroethane		Jr.	Junior
Dem.	Democrat		junc.	junction
dept.	department		kg.	kilogram
diag.	diagram		km.	kilometer
dict.	dictionary		l.	liter
dm.	decimeter		lab.	laboratory
doz.	dozen		lang.	language
Dr.	doctor		lat.	latitude
D.S.T.	Daylight Saving Time		lb.	pound
ed.	edition		leg.	legislature
educ.	education		lib.	librarian; library
			liq.	liquid
			lit.	literature
			Lt., Lieut.	Lieutenant

Ltd.	Limited	Prof.	Professor
m.	meter	prop.	property
M.A.	Master of Arts	Prov.	Proverbs
math	mathematics	P.S.	postscriptum, postscript
M.D.	Doctor of Medicine	P.S.T.	Pacific Standard Time
mdse.	merchandise	pt.	pint
meas.	measure	qt.	quart
memo	memorandum	rd.	road
mfg.	manufacturing	recd.	received
mfr., manuf.	manufacturer	ref.	reference; refer
min.	minute	reg.	region; regulation
misc.	miscellaneous	regt.	regiment
Mlle.	Mademoiselle	rep.	representative; republic
mi.	mile	Rev.	Reverend; Revelations
mm.	millimeter	rev.	review; revise; revolution
Mme.	Madame	R.I.P.	rest in peace
mo.	month	R.R.	railroad
Mon.	Monday	R.S.V.P.	Answer, if you please
mph	miles per hour	Sat.	Saturday
Msgr.	Monsignor	sch.	school
Mr.	Mister	sec.	second
Mrs.	Mistress	secy.	secretary
M.S.T.	Mountain Standard Time	sig.	signature
Mt., mt.	Mount; mountain	sing.	singular
mun.	municipal	sp.	spelling
Myth.	Mythology	spec.	specification
n.	noun; north	sq.	square
nat., natl.	national	Sr.	Senior
NATO	North Atlantic	St.	Saint; strait; street
	Treaty Organization	subj.	subject
no.	number	Sun.	Sunday
O.K.	correct; all right	Supt.	Superintendent
oz.	ounce	syn.	synonym
p.	page	t.	ton
par.	paragraph; parenthesis	tech.	technical; technology
parl.	parliament	temp.	temperature
pat.	patent	Thurs.	Thursday
pd.	paid	treas.	treasurer
Ph.D.	Doctor of Philosophy	Tues.	Tuesday
philos.	philosophy	UN	United Nations
phot., photog.	photograph	univ.	university
pk.	park; peak; peck	v.	verb
pl.	plural; place	vs.	versus, against
P.M., p.m.	post meridiem, afternoon;	vet.	veteran; veterinary
	postmaster; post-mortem	VIP	Very Important Person
P.O.	post office	vol.	volume
pop.	population	V.P.	Vice-President
POW	prisoner of war	Wed.	Wednesday
ppd.	prepaid	wk.	week
Pres.	President	wt.	weight
prin.	principal	yd.	yard
		yr.	year

SELECTED WORD LIST OF SYNONYMS, ANTONYMS, HOMONYMS AND HETERONYMS

Word	Synonym	Antonym	Homonym
above	over	below	—
absent	missing	present	—
abuse	mistreat	abet	—
add	total	subtract	—
adept	proficient	unskilled	—
adore	love	hate	—
advance	proceed	retreat	—
aid	help	hinder	ade, aide
air	atmosphere	earth	heir
aisle	passageway	blockade	isle
alike	same	different	—
all	everything	none	awl
alter	change	preserve	altar
ancient	old	modern	—
answer	reply	question	—
appear	emerge	disappear	—
arid	dry	wet	—
ate	consumed	fasted	eight
attach	fasten	remove	—
baby	infant	adult	—
back	rear	front	—
backward	reversed	forward	—
bad	evil	good	—
bare	naked	clothed	bear
basis	foundation	summit	bases
be	exist	isn't	bee
beat	defeat	win	beet
beautiful	lovely	ugly	—
been	was	wasn't	bin
before	formerly	after	—
begin	start	end	—
below	beneath	above	—
bend	curve	straighten	—
black	darkness	light	—
blew	gusted	calmed	blue
blunt	dull	sharp	—
bore	discontent	excite	boar
*bow	submit	refuse	bough
*bowl	dish	—	bole, boll
brave	courageous	frightened	—
break	shatter	repair	brake
bridal	wedding	—	bridle
bright	billiant	dim	—
brink	edge	center	—
bury	inter	unearth	berry
buy	purchase	sell	by, bye
calm	tranquil	excited	—

*heteronym

46

47

Word	Synonym	Antonym	Homonym
canvas	cloth	—	canvass
capital	principal	unimportant	capitol
cereal	porridge	—	serial
chief	leader	follower	—
choose	select	reject	—
city	metropolis	country	—
clever	smart	dumb	—
*close	shut	open	—
coarse	rough	smooth	course
cold	icy	hot	—
collect	gather	disperse	—
come	arrive	go	—
comic	funny	tragic	—
compliment	praise	criticize	complement
cool	chilly	warm	—
counsel	advise	—	council
creek	brook	—	creak
cry	weep	laugh	—
damage	impair	repair	—
danger	peril	safety	—
dark	unlit	light	—
day	daylight	night	—
dead	deceased	alive	—
dear	beloved	foe	deer
decrease	reduce	increase	—
deep	bottomless	shallow	—
*desert	abandon	retrieve	dessert
despise	hate	adore	—
die	decease	grow	dye
difficult	hard	easy	—
dirty	filthy	clean	—
disperse	distribute	gather	—
distant	far	near	—
dry	arid	wet	—
dull	boring	exciting	—
early	premature	late	—
elusive	evasive	overt	—
eminent	prominent	obscure	—
employ	hire	fire	—
empty	vacant	full	—
end	finish	begin	—
enemy	foe	friend	—
enlarge	expand	reduce	—
even	smooth	bumpy	—
exceed	excel	fail	—
except	barring	including	—

*heteronym

Word	Synonym	Antonym	Homonym
excess	abundant	sparse	—
exit	leave	enter	—
expand	swell	contract	—
export	send	import	—
fail	flop	succeed	—
fair	just	unfair	fare
fall	descend	rise	—
fat	obese	thin	—
feat	deed	—	feet
feeble	weak	strong	—
first	foremost	last	—
fix	repair	break	—
flower	blossom	—	flour
follow	pursue	lead	—
foolish	silly	wise	—
form	shape	shapeless	—
formerly	previously	presently	—
forth	forward	backward	fourth
frighten	terrify	soothe	—
funny	humorous	serious	—
fur	pelt	—	fir
future	approaching	past	—
gain	profit	loss	—
gamble	bet	—	gambol
gather	assemble	disburse	—
gaze	stare	glance	—
generous	unselfish	stingy	—
good	kindness	evil	—
great	large	small	grate
groan	moan	laugh	grown
halt	stop	start	—
hangar	shed	—	hanger
happy	glad	sad	—
hard	rigid	soft	—
hare	rabbit	—	hair
harmless	painless	harmful	—
hate	despise	love	—
heal	cure	infect	heel
healthy	well	ill	—
here	present	there	hear
heroine	victor	loser	heroin
hinder	obstruct	advance	—
holy	sacred	profane	wholly
homely	unattractive	pretty	—
hot	heated	cold	—
huge	large	tiny	—

*heteronym

48

Word	Synonym	Antonym	Homonym
hurl	throw	catch	—
idle	slothful	busy	idol, idyll
ill	sick	well	—
illusive	imaginary	real	—
imaginary	illusory	real	—
in	inside	outside	inn
inflate	expand	deflate	—
iniquity	wickedness	goodness	—
innocent	faultless	guilty	—
insight	discernment	—	incite
joy	happiness	sadness	—
keen	sharp	blunt	—
knave	rascal	gentleman	nave
knows	understands	(is) ignorant	nose
late	tardy	early	—
leak	crack	—	leek
leave	depart	return	—
led	guided	followed	*lead
like	same	different	—
*live	exist	die	—
little	small	big	—
lone	one	several	loan
loose	unfastened	tied	—
loud	noisy	quiet	—
low	inferior	superior	lo
made	created	destroyed	maid
male	man	woman	mail
mantle	cloak	—	mantel
medal	award	—	metal, mettle
meet	assemble	adjourn	meat
minor	petty	major	miner
missle	projectile	—	missal
more	additional	less	—
mourning	grief	gladness	morning
muscle	strength	weakness	mussel
narrow	thin	wide	—
native	indigenous	foreign	—
natural	normal	alien	—
neat	orderly	sloppy	—
necessary	obligatory	unnecessary	—
need	require	have	knead
new	contemporary	old	knew, gnu
night	evening	day	—
no	negative	yes	know
noisy	loud	quiet	—
none	nothing	all	nun
open	accessible	closed	—

*heteronym

49

Word	Synonym	Antonym	Homonym
pain	ache	comfort	pane
pair	twins	single	pare, pear
pale	pallid	rosy	pail
pallet	bedding	—	palette, palate
peace	tranquillity	upheaval	piece
peal	ring	—	peel
pin	fasten	undo	*pen
place	put	remove	plaice
plain	intelligible	confusing	plane
polite	courteous	rude	—
powerful	strong	weak	—
presence	proximity	absence	*presents
prey	quarry	predator	pray
principle	essential	unnecessary	principal
prohibit	forbid	permit	—
*project	protrude	recede	—
push	shove	pull	—
question	query	answer	—
raise	elevate	lower	raze
*read	peruse	—	reed
real	actual	fake	reel
red	florid	pale	read
*refuse	decline	accept	—
reign	rule	obey	rain
remain	stay	leave	—
rich	wealthy	poor	—
right	correct	wrong	wright, rite
ring	peal	—	wring
rode	drove	walked	road
rough	coarse	smooth	ruff
route	course	—	root, rout
rumor	gossip	truth	roomer
sad	unhappy	glad	—
same	identical	different	—
scene	setting	—	seen
scents	odors	—	cents
scream	yell	whisper	—
sea	ocean	—	see
seem	appear	is	seam
sell	vend	purchase	cell
sent	dispatched	returned	cent
serf	slave	master	surf
sheer	thin	opaque	shear
shy	timid	aggressive	—
sight	vision	blindness	site, cite
slow	unhurried	fast	sloe
small	tiny	large	—
smile	grin	frown	—
soar	fly	—	sore

*heteronym

Word	Synonym	Antonym	Homonym
sole	only	several	soul
some	few	many	sum
son	scion	daughter	sun
sour	acerbic	sweet	—
*sow	plant	reap	so, sew
speak	talk	listen	—
stake	peg	—	steak
stare	gaze	glance	stair
start	begin	stop	—
stationary	motionless	movable	stationery
steal	rob	buy	steel
straight	undeviating	curved	strait
stray	deviate	stay	—
strong	powerful	weak	—
stubborn	obstinate	yielding	—
tacks	nails	—	tax
take	remove	return	—
tale	fable	—	tail
tardy	late	punctual	—
taught	instructed	learned	taut
*tear	rip	mend	—
there	thereat	here	their, they're
threw	pitched	caught	through
time	interval	—	thyme
timid	shy	bold	—
to	toward	from	too, two
top	apex	bottom	—
tow	pull	push	toe
troupe	company	—	troop
true	certain	false	—
unique	original	common	—
usual	normal	rare	—
vacant	empty	full	—
vain	futile	warranted	vein, vane
vice	sin	virtue	—
wait	tarry	rush	weight
want	desire	need	—
waste	squander	conserve	waist
wave	ripple	—	waive
way	manner	—	weigh
weak	feeble	strong	week
wear	don	—	where
well	healthy	ill	—
whoa	stop	go	woe
whole	entire	part	hole
wild	savage	tame	—
*wind	breeze	—	—
won	succeeded	lost	one
wood	lumber	—	would
wry	crooked	straight	rye
you	thou	I	ewe, yew

*heteronym

IDIOMS

She bawled her eyes out.
My brother gets in my hair.
He lost his marbles.
The idea rang a bell.
He was burned up.
Go fly a kite.
He almost bit my head off!
She blew her stack.
He's on top of the world.
She is as quiet as a mouse.
He's as neat as a pin.
The baby is prettier than a picture.
He's like a bull in a china shop.
He is as ugly as a mud fence.
Money was as scarce as hens' teeth.
That will take him down a peg.
Dad will get wind of it.
Money always burns a hole in my pocket.
Will you lend me a hand?
She was so nervous that she blew the test.
I was so scared, I was shaking in my boots.
The girl was walking on air after the dance.
I was furious, but I held my tongue.
I'm between the devil and the deep blue sea.
He's not worth a hill of beans.
I think he bit off more than he can chew.
It's raining cats and dogs out there!
He has a trick up his sleeve.
It's as plain as the nose on your face.
I'm in a pretty pickle!
Do you have a skeleton in your closet?
The handwriting was on the wall.
She can really put on the dog.
He's a stool pigeon for the police.
I'm coming, so keep your shirt on.
He's tied to his mother's apron strings.
I'll stay until the bitter end.
He's talking through his hat.
That's right down my alley.
He is a pain in the neck.
The cowboy bit the dust.
He's as nutty as a fruitcake.
I have a splitting headache.
Put your John Hancock on the paper.
I never see eye to eye with you.

Is she ever in the dumps!
For crying out loud, stop that noise.
I have a bone to pick with you!
She really can chew the fat.
You just hit the nail on the head.
By hook or by crook, I'll get it.
That rings a bell with me.
The judge will throw the book at him.
Don't get your dander up.
It's nothing to shake a stick at.
Hold your horses!
I just had to blow off steam.
Keep a stiff upper lip.
I believe she is full of beans.
The teacher called him on the carpet.
That is as easy as rolling off a log.
I've got to get forty winks.
He has too many irons in the fire.
It was a long row to hoe.
She's as mad as a wet hen.
It's not fake, it's the real McCoy.
You're in the doghouse now!
That is just a drop in the bucket.
The doctor says I'm fit as a fiddle.
After winning the lottery, I'll be on Easy Street.
The storekeeper wanted cash on the barrel.
I broke the window, and I'm in hot water now!
He bought the company and then lost his shirt.
After the accident, things were touch and go.
You have to make hay while the sun shines.
What I say to him goes in one ear and out the other.
Don't make a mountain out of a molehill.
I'll keep my eye on the baby for you.
The dead fish smelled to high heaven.
I saw the snake and almost jumped out of my skin.
She goes hog wild getting ready for a party.
We played a game at the party to break the ice.
To clean that dirty oven, I have to use lots of elbow grease.
He cried wolf one too many times.
Don't cry over spilt milk.
You're skating on thin ice when you tell your mother a lie.
Are you getting cold feet about asking for more money?
Many sailors have gone to Davy Jones's locker.
He got into the party by crashing the gate.
He's just trying to keep up with the Joneses.

GREAT WAYS TO SHARE A BOOK

- Make a crossword puzzle using ideas from a book. Give the puzzle to someone who has read the book. Make enough copies to keep on hand for others who read the book.

- Read a book that has been made into a movie. Write an essay comparing the movie to the book.

- Rewrite the story as a picture book. Use simple vocabulary so that the book may be enjoyed by younger students.

- Suggest some changes which you think the author might make in order to improve the book.

- Dress up as one of the characters and tell the story from a first person viewpoint.

- After reading a book about history or a historical fiction, make a time line or calendar to show the important events of the story.

- Prepare a list of questions for use in determining if others have read the book carefully.

- Write a description of one of the main characters. Paint a portrait or caricature to accompany the description.

- Make three or four simple puppets of characters in the book. Prepare a short puppet show to tell the story to the class.

- Write a letter to the school librarian telling why she or he should recommend the book to other classes.

- Compare the illustrations of two books. Tell how the illustrations influence the reader.

- After reading a factual book, make a list of ten important facts you found in the book.

- Write a letter recommending the book to a friend or relative in another city.

- Write a book review to be printed in the school newspaper.

- Write a letter to the author of a book, telling your feelings about the story. Mail the letter to the book's publishing company.

- Make a map showing where the story took place.

- Write a diary from the main character's viewpoint to explain the events of the story.

- Make up three different endings for the story.

- Make a list of questions to ask someone who has read the same book. Then, interview that person and record his or her answers on tape.

- Write a letter to the main character of your book. (Ask a question, protest some situation, make a complaint or suggestion, etc.)

- Write a feature news article (with a headline) that tells the story as it might be found on the front page of a newspaper in the town where the story takes place.

- Draw several illustrations to accompany the book. Be prepared to tell the story to the class, using the pictures as aids.

- Make a travel poster inviting tourists to visit the setting of the book.

- If your book is a poetry book, make a scrapbook containing 15 or 20 of your favorite poems.

- After reading a joke and riddle book, make a scrapbook of original jokes and riddles.

- Make a diorama which shows the setting of a main event from the book.

- Make a poster which advertises your book.

From THE KIDS' STUFF™ BOOK OF READING AND LANGUAGE ARTS FOR THE MIDDLE GRADES, © 1987 by Incentive Publications, Inc., Nashville, TN. Used by permission.

READING SKILLS CHECKLIST

Student's Name   Grade   Date   Teacher's Name

I. WORD RECOGNITION SKILLS

PHONETIC ANALYSIS

____ Knows and uses long and short vowels, vowel teams, and vowel rules

____ Knows and uses consonant sounds, blends, and rules

____ Recognizes and understands functions of word endings and letter combinations that can be combined to form or change the sounds and/or meanings of words

____ Knows and can use phonetic symbols

____ Recognizes rhyming words

STRUCTURAL ANALYSIS

____ Knows and can use rules for syllabication

____ Recognizes and can expand root words

____ Knows and can use prefixes and suffixes

____ Can use contractions and abbreviations

____ Can use compound words

____ Can discriminate between words that look similar but are pronounced differently

____ Can interpret plurals and possessives

II. WORD USAGE SKILLS

WORD MEANING

____ Can use sight vocabulary

____ Can use picture clues

____ Can use context clues

____ Can define words by classification or function

___ Can understand multiple meanings of a given word
___ Recognizes and can use common synonyms, antonyms, and homonyms for familiar words
___ Recognizes and can use key words in content areas
___ Can interpret and convey meanings of a variety of familiar words

WORD SENSITIVITY

___ Can associate words with feelings
___ Can form sensory impressions
___ Can interpret figurative and idiomatic expressions
___ Can interpret sensations and moods suggested by words
___ Can recognize word relationships
___ Can recognize and use descriptive words
___ Is developing word appreciation

III. COMPREHENSION SKILLS

___ Can recall information read and select facts to remember
___ Can read for a specific purpose
___ Can find the main idea
___ Can read to find details
___ Can make comparisons and associations
___ Can classify material read
___ Can arrange ideas or events in sequence
___ Can summarize
___ Can read to verify answers
___ Can draw conclusions
___ Can make inferences
___ Can predict outcomes
___ Can make value judgements

___ Can distinguish between
    ___ relevant and irrelevant
    ___ fact and opinion
    ___ cause and effect
___ Is sensitive to author's purpose and mood
___ Can identify with fictional characters
___ Is sensitive to the development of plot and sequence
___ Can visualize

IV. READING STUDY SKILLS

___ Can use the dictionary
    ___ Can alphabetize
    ___ Can use guide words, symbols and keys
___ Can determine what reference source to use, and can use multiple resources related to one topic
    ___ thesaurus and encyclopedia
    ___ library materials
    ___ catalogs, magazines and newspapers
    ___ table of contents, index and glossary
___ Can read and use systematically organized materials
    ___ maps and globes
    ___ charts, tables, graphs and diagrams
___ Can understand and use punctuation
___ Can follow written directions
___ Can outline material read
___ Can take notes from reading
___ Can skim to locate facts and details
___ Can organize facts to support a conclusion
___ Is developing an increased reading rate, reading accuracy, and reading independence

WORD GAMES TO REINFORCE VOCABULARY

1. Use the successive letters of the alphabet as a determinate for creating a list of words having to do with any given subject. Two or more players may take turns. The first player not able to come up with an answer loses.

     Theme: Vegetables
     Examples: A—artichoke
                B—bean
                C—corn
                   etc.

2. Create an alphabetical list of words, each word containing a specified letter(s) in a specified position(s).

     Examples: <u>a</u> n a <u>t</u> o m y
                <u>b</u> r o <u>t</u> he r
                <u>c</u> a p <u>t</u> a i n

3. Have a contest with yourself or several contestants to see how many words containing a specified letter sequence can be listed.

Examples:	RTH	NTR	ACH
	birth	entry	reach
	earth	sentry	each
	north	untrue	machine

4. Create word mazes on a given theme. Use twenty squares. Find words by beginning in any square and moving from letter to letter in any direction (horizontally, vertically, or diagonally), until a word is completed. No letter may be used twice in succession (i.e. raccoon is not an answer).

     Example: Theme: ANIMALS

L	A	W	O	H
I	R	C	G	D
S	O	N	A	I
H	E	E	P	T

     Answers: dog, hog, cat, pig, sheep, horse, cow, lion

5. Create a game in which the object of the game is to discover the "rule" of the game. The player(s) may ask questions that can be answered with "yes" or "no." The literal meaning of the question is of no significance.

     Example: "Rule" of the game: Only questions whose last word begins with the letter "L" are acceptable.
     Thus: Does it have to be living? (Answer: yes)
            Are you lying? (Answer: yes)
            Was your last response true? (Answer: no)

By continuing to ask questions, player(s) deduce the criteria by which their questions are judged and discover the "rule" of the game.

6. A word category game, such as the one that follows, forces recall, application, and synthesis.

    Form a matrix which presents any five categories across the top and any five letters down the side. The object of the game is to supply one word which satisfies both factors. The game may be played against an opponent or against time. Change categories and letters for each game.

    Example:

	Animals	Games	Vegetables	Cities	Historical Figures
S	snake	Sorry	spinach	Savannah	Stalin
P	possum	Parcheesi	peas	Paducah	Patton
A					
F					
T					

7. Create a word game which fits the following format.

    Use a grid of twenty-five squares. Provide twenty-five letters (letters may be duplicated). The letters must be entered in the squares so as to form 2-, 3-, 4-, and 5-letter words which will read correctly both vertically and horizontally. Each letter must be used, and may be used only once. Each word is worth five points. Two points are subtracted for each letter not used. The player who has the most points wins.
    Example: E E N O T S P A P E O T L A E N R O S T A E E N E

S	T	R	A	P
	O			
	A			
	S			
	T			

8. Fluency in association is greatly stimulated by this game. Make two lists of words. Write them opposite each other with three or four blanks between them. Fill in the blanks so that each word across will have some meaningful relationship with the word preceding it and the word following it.
    Examples:

sour	lemon	twist	dance	shoe
cloud	rain	hat	Easter	rabbit
desk				view
cat				cry
race				trip

GLOSSARY OF TERMS RELATED TO
READING READINESS

Attention Span - the length of time that an individual's focus on a task can be sustained

Auditory Association - the ability to interpret, integrate, and use what is heard (the auditory world) in a meaningful way

Auditory Closure (sound blending) - the ability to blend sounds (given with time intervals) and identify the whole word

Auditory Discrimination - the ability to hear differences and similarities in sounds

Auditory Perception - the sensory ability to receive, arrange, and interpret auditory stimuli

Behavioral Objective - the specific competency to be achieved which is expressed in terms of the specific behavior the child needs to perform

Categorization - the ability to classify visual objects or auditory sounds in general groups

Competency - mastery of a skill

Comprehension - the ability to understand and integrate information in a meaningful manner

Conceptualization - general reasoning abilities, moving from the concrete to the abstract

Decoding Skills - receptive language (listening and reading with meaning)

Defining - the ability to express understanding of the spoken or written word — (1) concrete level - simple identification (naming) (2) functional level - defining words by their characteristics and by what they do (3) abstract level - classification and analogous situations

Developmental Level - the maturational stage at which the child is able to perform certain tasks

Directionality - the awareness of the body to points in space (including left and right, up and down, etc.)

Encoding Skills - expressive language skills (speaking and writing with meaning)

Expressive Language - words understood and used for meaningful communication

Eye-Hand Motor Coordination - the ability to integrate visual and motor skills

Figure Ground Skill Development - the visual ability to see objects and to separate them from their background; the auditory ability to listen to sounds without being distracted by the environment

Fine Motor Skills - movements requiring use of the small muscles of the body (writing, cutting, sewing, etc.)

Frustration Level - the difficulty level at which the child is unable to perform without undue anxiety

Gross Motor Skills - movements requiring the use of the large muscles of the body (hopping, running, jumping, etc.)

Identification (auditory and visual) - the ability to express recognition with vocal or motor response

Individualization - instruction designed for meeting specific developmental needs

Informal Prescriptive Teaching - individualizing instruction through observation, teacher evaluation, program planning, and implementation

Language - decoding, associating, and encoding visual and auditory symbols (language assumes comprehension)

Localization (auditory) - locating the direction of a sound

Mainstreaming - the educational movement to place children who have been in special classes in the regular classroom setting

Memory - the ability to store and recall information after the stimulus has been removed

Nonverbal Language - attaching meaning to visual and auditory information through gestures, expressions, intonations and subtleties

Phoneme (phonics) - the smallest unit of sound in language

Phonics - the science of sound; applying sound to the written word

Readiness Skills - the pre-academic, developmental skills necessary for reading and writing success

Reading - a receptive language skill requiring the ability to associate the visual symbol (the written word) with its appropriate unit of experience

Receptive Language - understanding visual and auditory information

Receptive Vocabulary - the fund of words understood by the child

Rhyming - the ability to hear similarities in word endings

Sequential Memory - the ability to recall information in the same sequence given

Spatial Design - the ability to see and reproduce designs in a given space

Verbal Association - the ability to interpret, integrate, and use what is seen (the visual world) in a meaningful way

Verbal Fluency - the ability to express oneself vocally

Visual Closure - the ability to fill in the missing parts to make a whole

Visual Discrimination - the ability to see differences and similarities in visual objects, pictures, and symbols

Visual Perception - the sensory ability to receive, organize, and interpret visual stimuli

Visual Relationships - the ability to understand the relationships among objects, pictures, and symbols

NOTES